# CHEESE

# CHEESE

*Sumptuous cheese recipes for all occasions*

ISBN: 978-1-4075-9682-2

Printed in China

Design concept by Fiona Roberts
Produced by the Bridgewater Book Company Ltd
Photographer: David Jordan
Home Economist: Jacqueline Bellefontaine

**Notes for the Reader**

This book uses imperial, metric, and US cup measurements. Follow the same units of measurement throughout; do not mix imperial and metric. All spoon measurements are level: teaspoons are assumed to be 5 ml, and tablespoons are assumed to be 15 ml. Unless otherwise stated, milk is assumed to be whole, eggs and individual vegetables such as potatoes are medium, and pepper is freshly ground black pepper.

The times given are an approximate guide only. Preparation times differ according to the techniques used by different people and the cooking times may also vary from those given as a result of the type of oven used. Optional ingredients, variations or serving suggestions have not been included in the calculations.

Recipes using raw or very lightly cooked eggs should be avoided by infants, the elderly, pregnant women, convalescents, and anyone with a chronic condition. Pregnant and breastfeeding women are advised to avoid eating peanuts and peanut products. Sufferers from nut allergies should be aware that some of the ready-prepared ingredients used in the recipes in this book may contain nuts. Always check the packaging before use.

# contents

# Introduction

CHEESE IS, OF COURSE, THE ULTIMATE FAST FOOD. PURISTS WOULD ARGUE THAT TO TRULY APPRECIATE THE FLAVOR OF GOOD CHEESE IT SHOULD BE EATEN COMPLETELY UNADULTERATED ON ITS OWN WITH A KNIFE AND FORK. THIS MAY BE TRUE, AND A WELL-CONSIDERED CHEESEBOARD OFFERING A VARIETY OF PERFECTLY RIPE CHEESES NEEDS LITTLE MORE THAN GOOD-QUALITY BREAD AND A GLASS OF WINE. HOWEVER, ONLY TO EAT CHEESE ON ITS OWN WOULD BE TO MISS OUT ON ITS INFINITE VARIETY AND VERSATILITY AS A COOKING INGREDIENT. THERE ARE SOME CHEESES THAT REALLY COME INTO THEIR OWN IN COOKING AND INDEED WOULD BE OUT OF PLACE AS PART OF A CHEESEBOARD, SUCH AS PROVOLONE, RICOTTA, AND FETA CHEESE. SIMILARLY, THERE ARE SOME CHEESES THAT ARE TRADITIONALLY ONLY USED IN COOKING BUT WHICH ARE DELICIOUS EATEN WITH A PIECE OF FRUIT AND BREAD OR CRACKERS—PARMESAN OR ROMANO CHEESE, FOR INSTANCE.

There is now an ever-expanding number of cheeses available, giving us the opportunity to use as many as possible in cooking. It is also well worth experimenting with using different cheeses in familiar recipes, as long as you choose the right type of cheese for the dish.

This book offers recipes for all-time favorites such as Macaroni Cheese and Croque Monsieur as well as more adventurous recipes that feature a wide variety of cheeses. Take care to note which particular type of cheese is specified in each recipe. For instance, if a goat cheese is required, make sure you are aware whether it's a soft cheese with no rind, a chèvre with a milky, soft rind, or even a sharp hard goat cheese. The important issue is the particular properties of the cheese, and it is usually possible to substitute another cheese provided it has the same basic qualities.

For a quick bite or a palate tickler, nothing beats cheese. Very simple yet tasty cheesy morsels can be put together in no time. A tender sautéed portobello mushroom topped with a slice of provolone cheese, brown and bubbling from the broiler, is one such delight. Alternatively, wrap a finger of feta in a sheet of lightly oiled phyllo pastry and bake in a hot oven for 10 minutes. Or beat chopped fresh herbs or crushed black peppercorns into soft goat cheese and serve as a dip with crudités and cocktails, or add some beaten eggs and herbs to ricotta cheese and bake in the oven for a light snack.

But if you are looking for something a little more sophisticated, choose from this varied selection of imaginative ideas for all kinds of occasion, drawn from around the world. From Spain come golden saffron pastries encasing a delicious duo of manchego

# CHEESE WITH EASE

cheese and quince paste, and from Greece, delightfully crisp feta-flavored Walnut Cheese Wafers—both perfect for party food, along with Italian-inspired Parmesan Crackers with Walnut Pesto. And see what sumptuous snacks can be created from the humble cheese sandwich—Fried Cheese Sandwiches, oozing with molten mozzarella, also from Italy, and that great French bistro classic, the Croque Monsieur, made with fruity-flavored Gruyère or Emmental cheese. Also from France are crêpes enriched with a creamy goat cheese and leek filling, seasoned with fresh chives and nutmeg.

SERVES 4

7 oz/200 g mozzarella di bufala

8 x ½-inch/1-cm thick slices day-old
white bread, crusts removed

6 tbsp unsalted butter

4 medium slices Italian salami

corn oil, for deep-frying

3 eggs

3 tbsp milk

salt and pepper

TOMATO SAUCE

3 tbsp olive oil

1 onion, chopped

2 garlic cloves, minced

1 red bell pepper, seeded and
chopped

14 oz/400 g canned tomatoes,
chopped

2 tbsp tomato paste

1 tbsp lemon juice

2 tbsp water

salt and pepper

# Fried Cheese Sandwiches with Tomato Sauce

This Neapolitan specialty is one of the nicest ways to serve mozzarella cheese. It makes a wonderful snack for 2 people, as well as a superb appetizer for 4.

• First, make the sauce. Heat the olive oil in a medium, heavy-bottom pan and cook the onion and garlic, stirring frequently, for 5 minutes, or until soft. Add the red bell pepper and cook, stirring frequently, for an additional 5 minutes. Stir in the tomatoes, tomato paste, lemon juice, and water and season to taste with salt and pepper. Cover and simmer for 15 minutes, or until pulpy.

• Meanwhile, slice the cheese into 4 thick or 8 medium slices. Spread the bread slices with the butter and place the cheese on 4 of them. Top with the salami and sandwich together with the remaining bread slices. Cut in half to make triangles, then wrap in plastic wrap and let chill in the refrigerator.

• Remove the sauce from the heat and let cool slightly, then process in a food processor or blender until smooth. Return the sauce to a clean pan and reheat gently.

• Preheat the oven to 325°F/160°C. Heat the corn oil in a deep, heavy-bottom pan or deep-fryer to 350–375°F/180–190°C, or until a cube of bread browns in 30 seconds. Meanwhile, beat the eggs with the milk in a shallow dish and season to taste with salt and pepper. Unwrap the sandwiches and dip them, in batches, into the egg mixture, letting them soak briefly. Add the sandwiches, in batches, to the hot oil and cook until golden brown on both sides. Remove with tongs and drain on paper towels. Transfer to a warmed plate and keep warm in the preheated oven while you cook the remaining triangles. Serve the sandwiches hot and hand round the sauce separately.

MAKES 2

3½ oz/100 g Gruyère or Emmental
    cheese, grated
4 slices white bread, with the
    crusts trimmed
2 thick slices ham
1 small egg, beaten
3 tbsp unsalted butter, plus extra
    if necessary

WHITE SAUCE

2 tbsp unsalted butter
1 tsp corn oil
½ tbsp all-purpose flour
½ cup warm milk
pepper

# Croque Monsieur

For a croque madame, add a fried egg to the ham and cheese filling. For a more robust flavor, spread the bread with dijon or whole grain mustard before adding the ham and cheese.

• Spread half the cheese on 2 bread slices, then top each with a slice of ham, cut to fit. Sprinkle the ham with all but 2 tablespoons of the remaining cheese, then sandwich together with the remaining bread slices and press down well.

• To make the sauce, melt the butter with the oil in a small, heavy-bottom pan and stir in the flour until well combined and smooth. Cook over medium heat, stirring constantly, for 1 minute. Remove from the heat and stir in a little of the milk until well incorporated. Return to the heat and gradually add the remaining milk, stirring constantly, until it has all been incorporated. Cook for an additional 3 minutes, or until the sauce is smooth and thickened. Stir in the remaining cheese and pepper to taste, then set aside and keep warm.

• Beat the egg in a shallow dish. Add 1 sandwich and press down to coat on both sides, then remove from the dish and repeat with the other sandwich.

• Preheat the broiler to high. Line a cookie sheet with foil and set aside. Melt the butter in a sauté pan or skillet and cook 1 or both sandwiches, depending on the size of your pan, over medium-high heat until golden brown on both sides. Add a little extra butter, if necessary, if you have to cook the sandwiches separately.

• Transfer the sandwiches to the foil-lined cookie sheet and spread the white sauce over the top. Cook under the broiler, about 4 inches/10 cm from the heat, for 4 minutes, or until golden and brown.

SERVES 4

1 large eggplant, thinly sliced
   lengthwise
5 tbsp olive oil
scant ½ cup black olives, pitted
1 tbsp capers

scant 1 cup sun-dried tomatoes
2 garlic cloves
2 tbsp flat-leaf parsley, chopped
1 tsp lemon juice
6 oz/175 g provolone cheese,
   cut into sticks

# Broiled Eggplants with Provolone and Tapenade

You can use ready prepared tapenade or pistou rather than make your own, or simply spread the eggplants with a little harissa paste or garlic sesame seed paste (tahini) before adding the cheese.

• Preheat the oven to 425°F/220°C. Brush the eggplant slices with 2 tablespoons of the oil and place on a cookie sheet. Bake the eggplants in the preheated oven for 10 minutes, or until soft. Let cool.

• Meanwhile, put the olives, capers, tomatoes, garlic, and half the parsley in a food processor and pulse until coarsely chopped, or chop by hand. Add 2 tablespoons of the remaining oil and all the lemon juice and pulse to a smooth paste, or beat into the olive mixture by hand.

• Preheat the broiler to high. When the eggplants are cold, spread each one with a little of the tapenade. Place 2 of the cheese sticks at the end of each eggplant slice, then roll up and secure with a toothpick.

• Brush the eggplant rolls with the remaining oil and cook under the broiler, turning once, until golden brown and the cheese is beginning to melt.

• Serve scattered with the remaining parsley.

MAKES 12

½ tsp saffron threads

¾ cup tepid water

2⅓ cups all-purpose flour,
    plus extra for dusting

½ envelope active dry yeast

⅓ cup vegetable oil,
    plus extra for oiling

½ tsp sea salt

2 tbsp olive oil

1 onion, minced

½ tsp smoked paprika

9 oz/250 g manchego or
    almodovar cheese, cubed

2½ oz/70 g membrillo
    (quince paste), cubed

1 small egg, beaten with 1 tsp water,
    for glazing

# Manchego and Membrillo Saffron Pastries

If you cannot find membrillo, you could use apple jelly instead or another fruit paste.

• Mix the saffron with the water in a pitcher and let infuse for 1 minute. Meanwhile, put the flour, yeast, and vegetable oil in a large bowl. Add the saffron and its soaking liquid with the salt. Using a wooden spoon or floured hands, mix well to form a dough.

• Turn the dough out onto a floured counter and knead for 5 minutes, or until smooth and elastic. Transfer the dough to a lightly oiled bowl, cover with plastic wrap, and let stand in a warm place to rise for 1½ hours.

• Heat the olive oil in a nonstick skillet and cook the onion over low heat, stirring occasionally, for 15 minutes, or until the onion is very soft but not colored. Add the paprika and cook, stirring, for an additional 2 minutes, then remove from the heat. Mix the cheese and membrillo with the onion.

• Preheat the oven to 375°F/190°C. Turn the risen dough out onto the floured counter and knead briefly, then divide into 12 pieces. Roll each piece of dough into a circle and divide the filling between the dough circles. Brush the edges of the dough circles with some of the beaten egg and fold over, expelling all the air, to form a half moon shape. Using a fork, press the edges together, then trim to neaten and brush with the remaining beaten egg. Place on a lightly oiled cookie sheet.

• Cook in the preheated oven for 20 minutes, or until golden. Let cool on a cooling rack. Serve warm or cold.

MAKES 12

butter, for greasing

1 lb 2 oz/500 g prepared
   unsweetened pastry

all-purpose flour, for dusting

2 tbsp whole grain mustard

12 lean bacon slices, diced, cooked,
   and drained well

12 small eggs

1¼ cups grated Cheddar cheese

2 tbsp chopped fresh parsley

pepper

# Mini Bacon and Egg Pastries with Cheddar

Take care not to force the pastry circles into the muffin pans by stretching them, as this will lead to the pastry shrinking while it is in the oven. Gently ease the pastry into the pan so that it fits into the edges before filling the pastries.

• Preheat the oven to 350°F/180°C. Lightly grease a deep 12-hole muffin pan.

• Roll the pastry out to ¼ inch/5 mm thick on a lightly floured counter and cut out 12 circles about 5 inches/13 cm in diameter. Use to line the holes of the prepared muffin pan, gently pleating the sides of the dough as you ease it into the molds. Put ½ teaspoon of the mustard in the base of each pastry shell and top with a little of the bacon.

• Break an egg into a cup and spoon the yolk into a pastry shell, then add enough of the white to fill the pastry shell about two-thirds full. Do not overfill. Season to taste with pepper and sprinkle a little of the cheese evenly over the top. Repeat with the remaining pastry shells.

• Bake in the preheated oven for 20–25 minutes, or until the egg is set and the cheese is golden brown. Serve warm, sprinkled with the parsley.

MAKES 8
CRÊPES
generous ¾ cup all-purpose flour
pinch of salt
2 large eggs
1¼ cups milk
2 tbsp butter, melted and cooled
corn oil

FILLING
2 tbsp unsalted butter
½ tbsp corn oil
7 oz/200 g leeks, halved
    and finely shredded

freshly grated nutmeg, to taste
1 tbsp finely snipped fresh chives
3 oz/85 g soft goat cheese, rind
    removed if necessary, chopped
salt and pepper

# Leek and Goat Cheese Crêpes

Alternative ways of serving these crêpes include rolling them around reheated ratatouille, or grating fresh Parmesan cheese over their tops before putting them in the oven.

• To make the crêpe batter, sift the flour and salt into a large bowl and make a deep well in the center. Add the eggs and a little of the milk to the well and beat together, gradually drawing in the flour from the side. Stir in the butter, then gradually add the remaining milk until the batter has the consistency of light cream, stirring constantly to prevent lumps forming.

• Cover and let stand for at least 30 minutes. You can leave the batter in the refrigerator for up to 24 hours, but remember to remove it at least 15 minutes before cooking.

• Preheat the oven to 400°F/200°C. Melt the butter with the oil in a heavy-bottom pan over medium-high heat. Add the leeks and stir around so that they are well coated in the butter mixture. Add salt and pepper to taste, but remember that the cheese might be salty. Add a few gratings of nutmeg, then cover the leeks with a sheet of wet waxed paper and cover the pan. Reduce the heat to very low and leave the leeks to sweat for 5–7 minutes, or until very tender but not browned. Stir in the chives, then taste and adjust the seasoning if necessary.

• Give the batter another good beating. Heat an 8-inch/20-cm crêpe pan or skillet over high heat, then very lightly wipe the surface with corn oil, using a crumpled piece of paper towel.

• Reduce the heat to medium. Ladle 1½ fl oz/45 ml or 3 tablespoons of the batter into the center of the pan and immediately swirl the batter around so that it covers the bottom thinly.

• Cook for 1 minute, or until the underside is golden brown and the edge is golden. Using a metal spatula, flip the crêpe over and cook on the other side.

• Slide the crêpe onto the counter and put one-eighth of the leeks into the center, then top with one-eighth of the cheese and fold the crêpe into a square pocket or simply roll it around the filling. Place the filled crêpe on a cookie sheet. Repeat with the remaining batter, leeks, and cheese.

• Bake in the preheated oven for 5 minutes, or until the crêpes are hot and the cheese is beginning to melt. Remove from the oven and serve hot.

SERVES 4

4 large potatoes, such as long white
    potatoes, halved

7 oz/200 g soft rindless goat cheese,
    such as Chavroux

1 small fresh red chili,
    seeded and minced

½ tsp finely grated lemon rind

1 onion, thinly sliced

2 fresh thyme sprigs, leaves only

olive oil

salt and pepper

# Potato and Thyme Rösti with Soft Goat Cheese and Chili

You can add other ingredients to the rösti, such as grated apple or celery root for variety. If you don't like chili, just substitute some chopped fresh herbs such as chervil.

• Preheat the oven to 325°F/160°C. Cook the potatoes in a large pan of boiling water for 5 minutes. Drain in a colander and cover with a clean dish towel to absorb the steam. Let cool.

• Mash the cheese with the chili, lemon rind, and salt and pepper to taste in a large bowl. Cover and chill in the refrigerator until required.

• Grate the potatoes into a separate large bowl, then add the onion, salt and pepper to taste, and half the thyme and mix well.

• Heat 1 tablespoon of oil in a nonstick skillet. Place a tablespoon of the potato mixture in the skillet and flatten to form a rösti. Repeat with another 1–2 tablespoons of the potato mixture—don't overcrowd the skillet. Cook for 2–3 minutes, adding more oil if necessary, then carefully turn over and cook on the other side for 3 minutes until both sides are crisp. Drain on paper towels, then transfer to a warmed plate and keep warm in the preheated oven while you cook the remaining rösti.

• Place 2 rösti on each serving plate. Top each one with a good spoonful of the cheese mixture and serve immediately, garnished with the remaining thyme.

These recipes show just how versatile cheese can be as an ingredient, used in soup and salads, or as an ideal partner to baked or roasted Mediterranean vegetables. Even the humble potato can be enlivened by the addition of cheese—try mashing soft bleu Gorgonzola, snipped fresh chives, and an egg into the flesh of a baked potato and returning to the oven for 5 more minutes.

Cheese often makes a welcome appearance in salads, including the classic "tricolore" of mozzarella, tomato, and avocado—use traditionally made mozzarella di bufala from buffalo's milk for a superior result—and the famous Caesar salad, with grated Parmesan cheese—look for Parmigiano Reggiano on the rind for the authentic product. But here you can sample very different flavor combinations—creamy bleu Gorgonzola cheese teamed with fragrant ripe pear, crunchy walnuts, and slightly bitter

# LUXURIOUS LUNCHES

chicory, or aromatically spiced warm Puy lentils topped with meltingly broiled goat cheese. Bleu cheese and soft goat cheese also make excellent dressings, mashed or blended with mayonnaise thinned with heavy cream.

There are other winning combinations to enjoy in this chapter, such as juicy portobello mushrooms stuffed with fennel, sun-dried tomatoes, and mild yet distinctively flavored fontina cheese topped with grainy Parmesan cheese shavings, or crisp phyllo pastry enveloping sharp-tasting feta cheese and spinach. But for a real cheese feast for a special lunch with friends, go for a fun fondue featuring a range of cheeses laced with white wine and brandy.

SERVES 4

scant 4 tbsp butter

2 onions, chopped

1 potato, diced

3¾ cups hot vegetable
   or chicken stock

1 broccoli crown, broken
   into small florets

⅔ cup heavy cream, plus 3 tbsp

7 oz/200 g bleu cheese, crumbled

¼ oz/10 g fresh chives, snipped

pepper

# Broccoli and Cheese Soup

To make bleu cheese croûtes, brush slices of French stick with olive oil and toast in a low oven until golden. Mash the cheese with only 1 tablespoon cream and spread onto the toasted bread. Float a croûte in each bowl of soup.

• Heat the butter in a large pan and cook the onions, stirring frequently, for 5–8 minutes, or until soft. Stir in the potato, then add the hot stock and bring to a boil. Reduce the heat and simmer for 5 minutes.

• Add the broccoli and cook, stirring occasionally, for an additional 5 minutes. Season to taste with pepper. Transfer the soup to a blender or food processor, in batches, and process until smooth. Return to a clean pan.

• Add the ⅔ cup cream and three-quarters of the cheese to the soup and cook over low heat, stirring, until the cheese has melted.

• Mash the remaining cheese with the remaining cream.

• Serve the soup hot in individual warmed bowls with a good spoonful of the cheese and cream mixture, sprinkled with a few chives.

SERVES 4
1 garlic clove, peeled and halved
generous 1¾ cups dry white wine
5 tbsp brandy
7 oz/200 g Gruyère cheese, grated
7 oz/200 g Emmental cheese, grated

7 oz/200 g Comté cheese, grated
100 g/3½ oz Parmesan cheese, grated
2 tbsp cornstarch
pinch of freshly grated nutmeg
salt and pepper

DIPPERS
fresh crusty bread, cut into bite-size pieces
small pieces of blanched asparagus

# Swiss-Style Fondue with Brandy

The Swiss and French cheeses in this recipe are very similar. When choosing them, avoid any that have too many holes or are bulging. However, signs of moisture around the holes indicate that they are in good condition.

• Rub the inside of an ovenproof fondue pot with the garlic. Discard the garlic. Pour in the wine and 3 tablespoons of the brandy, then transfer to the stove and bring to a gentle simmer over low heat.

• Mix the cheeses together. Add a small handful of cheese to the fondue pot and stir constantly until melted. Continue to add the cheese gradually, stirring constantly after each addition. Repeat until all the cheese has been added and stir until thoroughly melted and bubbling gently.

• Mix the cornstarch with the remaining brandy in a bowl. Stir the cornstarch mixture into the fondue and cook, stirring constantly, for 3–4 minutes, or until thickened and bubbling. Stir in the nutmeg and season to taste with salt and pepper.

• Using protective gloves, transfer the fondue pot to a lit tabletop burner. To serve, encourage your guests to spear pieces of crusty bread and blanched asparagus onto fondue forks and dip them into the fondue.

SERVES 4

2½ cups water

2½ cups milk

1 tsp sea salt

½ tsp ground nutmeg

10½ oz/300 g fine polenta

¼ cup finely grated Parmesan cheese

5½ oz/150 g raclette or Mahon cheese, cubed

scant 4 tbsp unsalted butter, plus extra for greasing

2 fresh thyme sprigs, leaves only

pepper

green salad, to serve

# Baked Polenta with Cheese and Thyme

You may like to try adding a couple of extra ingredients to this dish—some sautéed mushrooms or a few crisp lardons can be scattered over the polenta before it goes into the oven.

• Put the water and milk in a large pan and bring to a boil over high heat. Add the salt, pepper to taste, and nutmeg, then pour in the polenta, stirring constantly. Reduce the heat to medium and cook, stirring constantly, for an additional 25–30 minutes, or until thick and pulling away from the sides of the pan.

• Remove from the heat and add the Parmesan cheese and half the raclette cheese and butter. Stir until melted and well combined.

• Pour the polenta onto a cold, nonstick cookie sheet, then spread out to ½ inch/1 cm thick and let cool completely.

• Meanwhile, preheat the oven to 400°F/200°C. Grease a shallow ceramic baking dish. Using a plain cookie cutter, cut out 2-inch/5-cm circles of the polenta and arrange, overlapping, in the prepared baking dish.

• Dice the remaining butter and cheese, then scatter over the polenta with the thyme leaves.

• Bake in the preheated oven for 15 minutes, or until golden and crisp. Serve with a green salad.

SERVES 6

2 tbsp olive oil

1 large onion, minced

2 lb 4 oz/1 kg fresh young spinach
   leaves or 1 lb 2 oz/500 g frozen
   spinach, thawed

4 tbsp chopped fresh flat-leaf parsley

2 tbsp chopped fresh dill

3 eggs, beaten

7 oz/200 g authentic Greek feta
   cheese (drained weight)

7/8 stick butter

8 oz/225 g authentic Greek
   phyllo pastry

salt and pepper

# Spanakópita

Try substituting ricotta cheese for feta cheese, then omit the eggs and replace some of the quantity with minced smoked ham.

• To make the filling, heat the oil in a pan and cook the onion, stirring frequently, for 5 minutes, or until soft. Add the fresh spinach, if using, with only the water clinging to the leaves after washing, or the frozen spinach, and cook for 2–5 minutes, or until wilted. Remove from the heat and let cool.

• When the mixture has cooled, add the parsley, dill, and eggs. Crumble in the cheese, then season to taste with salt and pepper and mix well together.

• Preheat the oven to 375°F/190°C. Melt the butter in a separate pan and use a little to lightly grease a deep 12- x 8-inch/30- x 20-cm roasting pan.

• Cut the pastry sheets in half widthwise. Take 1 sheet of pastry and cover the remaining sheets with a damp dish towel. Line the pan with the pastry sheet and brush it with a little of the remaining melted butter. Repeat with half the pastry sheets, brushing each with butter.

• Spread the spinach and cheese filling over the pastry, then top with the remaining pastry sheets, brushing each with butter and tucking down the edges. Using a sharp knife, score the top layers of the pastry into 6 squares.

• Bake in the preheated oven for 40 minutes, or until golden brown. Serve hot or cold.

SERVES 6–8

3 eggplants, thinly sliced

olive oil, for brushing

10½ oz/300 g mozzarella di bufala,
    sliced

generous 1 cup freshly grated
    Parmesan cheese

3 tbsp dried, uncolored bread crumbs

1 tbsp butter

salt

fresh flat-leaf parsley sprigs,
    to garnish

TOMATO AND BASIL SAUCE

2 tbsp virgin olive oil

4 shallots, minced

2 garlic cloves, minced

14 oz/400 g canned tomatoes

1 tsp sugar

8 fresh basil leaves, shredded

salt and pepper

# Eggplants with Mozzarella and Parmesan

This makes a delicious accompaniment to plainly cooked chicken, pork, or veal and can also be served with salad as a vegetarian entrée for 4 people.

• To remove any bitterness, layer the eggplant slices in a colander, sprinkling each layer with salt. Stand the colander in the sink and let drain for 30 minutes. Rinse thoroughly under cold running water to remove all traces of salt, then pat dry with paper towels.

• Meanwhile, preheat the oven to 400°F/200°C. Arrange the eggplant slices in a single layer on 1–2 large cookie sheets. Brush with olive oil and bake in the preheated oven for 15–20 minutes, or until tender but not collapsing.

• Meanwhile, make the sauce. Heat the virgin olive oil in a heavy-bottom pan and cook the shallots, stirring frequently, for 5 minutes, or until soft. Add the garlic and cook, stirring, for an additional minute. Add the tomatoes with their can juices and break up with a wooden spoon. Stir in the sugar and season to taste with salt and pepper. Bring to a boil, then reduce the heat and simmer for 10 minutes, or until thickened. Stir in the basil.

• Brush an ovenproof dish with olive oil and arrange half the eggplant slices in the base. Cover with half the mozzarella cheese, then spoon over half the sauce and sprinkle with half the Parmesan cheese. Mix the remaining Parmesan cheese with the bread crumbs. Make more layers, ending with the Parmesan cheese and bread crumb mixture.

• Dot the top with the butter and bake in the preheated oven for 25 minutes, or until the topping is golden brown. Remove from the oven and let stand for 5 minutes before slicing and serving, garnished with the parsley.

SERVES 4

2¼ cups fresh white bread crumbs

3 tbsp all-purpose flour

2 large eggs, beaten

9 oz/250 g Camembert cheese,
   cut into wedges and chilled

4 cups vegetable oil

fresh parsley sprigs, to garnish

CRANBERRY SAUCE

finely grated rind and juice of
   1 orange

½ cup superfine sugar

7 oz/200 g fresh cranberries

½ apple, peeled, cored, and diced

1 tbsp port (optional)

# Deep-Fried Camembert with Cranberry Sauce

You can substitute red currants for the cranberries if you prefer, or use a little orange liqueur instead of port in the sauce.

• To make the sauce, put the orange rind and juice and sugar in a pan and heat over low heat, stirring, until the sugar has dissolved. Stir in the cranberries, apple, and port, if using, and cook, uncovered, for 8–10 minutes, or until thick. Remove from the heat and let cool.

• Put the bread crumbs, flour, and eggs separately onto 3 plates. Coat each cheese wedge first in the flour and next in the egg, then in the bread crumbs and again in the egg.

• Preheat the oven to 325°F/160°C. Heat the oil in a deep, heavy-bottom pan or deep-fryer to 350–375°F/180–190°C, or until a cube of bread browns in 30 seconds. Cook the wedges, in batches of 2, for 3–4 minutes, or until crisp and golden brown. Remove with a slotted spoon and drain on paper towels. Transfer to a warmed plate and keep warm in the preheated oven while you cook the remaining wedges. Serve the wedges hot with the sauce, garnished with parsley.

SERVES 6

6 small red bell peppers

2 tbsp olive oil, plus extra for oiling

3 garlic cloves, thinly sliced

9 oz/250 g halloumi cheese,
  thinly sliced

12 fresh mint leaves

grated rind and juice of 1 lemon

1 tbsp chopped fresh thyme

3 tbsp pine nuts

pepper

# Roasted Red Bell Peppers with Halloumi

Provolone or feta can be used as an alternative to the halloumi cheese if preferred.

• Preheat the oven to 400°F/200°C. Cut the red bell peppers in half lengthwise and remove the cores and seeds. Rub the skins of the bell peppers with a little of the oil, then arrange the bell peppers, skin-side down, on a large oiled cookie sheet.

• Scatter half the garlic over the bell peppers. Top with the cheese, then scatter over the mint, lemon rind, remaining garlic, thyme, pine nuts, and pepper to taste. Drizzle over the remaining oil and the lemon juice.

• Roast the bell peppers in the preheated oven for 30 minutes, or until tender and beginning to char around the edges. Serve warm.

SERVES 4

2 tbsp corn oil, plus extra for oiling

12 large portobello mushrooms,
  stems removed

1 fennel bulb, stems removed,
  minced

3½ oz/100 g sun-dried tomatoes,
  minced

2 garlic cloves, crushed

4½ oz/125 g fontina cheese, grated

scant ½ cup freshly grated
  Parmesan cheese

3 tbsp chopped fresh basil

1 tbsp olive oil

salt and pepper

TO SERVE

fresh Parmesan cheese shavings

1 tbsp chopped fresh parsley

# Stuffed Portobello Mushrooms
# with Shaved Parmesan

Mushrooms absorb water, so never soak them to clean them. The best way to clean them is to wipe them over with a damp cloth. To make Parmesan cheese shavings, run a vegetable peeler down the side of the piece of cheese.

• Preheat the oven to 350°F/180°C. Lightly oil a large ovenproof dish. Arrange 8 of the mushrooms, cup-side up, in the dish and mince the remaining 4 mushrooms.

• Heat the corn oil in a nonstick skillet and cook the chopped mushrooms, fennel, tomatoes, and garlic over low heat, stirring occasionally, until soft but not browned. Remove from the heat and let cool.

• When cool, add the cheeses, basil, and salt and pepper to taste. Mix well. Brush the mushrooms lightly with the olive oil and fill each cavity with a spoonful of the vegetable mixture. Bake in the preheated oven for 20–25 minutes, or until the mushrooms are tender and the filling is heated through. Top with Parmesan cheese shavings and parsley and serve immediately, allowing 2 mushrooms for each person.

SERVES 4

3 tbsp pear or apple juice

2 tbsp walnut oil

1 tbsp finely snipped fresh chives

1 tsp white wine vinegar

1 tsp flower honey

3 ripe pears, Comice or similar,
  cored and sliced

juice of ½ lemon

2 red or green chicory heads

5½ oz/150 g corn salad

scant ¾ cup walnut pieces

7 oz/200 g Gorgonzola cheese,
  cubed or sliced

salt and white pepper

warm ciabatta bread, to serve
  (optional)

# Pear, Gorgonzola, and Walnut Salad

Radicchio also works well in this salad—it is best to choose a bitter leaf like chicory or radicchio to balance the sweetness of the fruit.

• To make the dressing, put the pear juice, oil, chives, vinegar, and honey in a screw-top jar, screw on the lid, and shake vigorously. Season to taste with salt and pepper.

• Toss the pear slices in the lemon juice to prevent browning.

• Separate the chicory heads into leaves. Arrange the chicory leaves with the corn salad on 4 individual plates and divide the pear slices, walnuts, and cheese between them. Pour over the dressing and serve with warm ciabatta bread, if using.

SERVES 4

1 tbsp olive oil, plus extra
  for brushing
2 red onions, finely sliced
2 garlic cloves, crushed
1 fresh red chili, seeded and minced
½ tsp turmeric
½ tsp ground cumin
½ tsp ground coriander
1 cinnamon stick
2 star anise
5 cardamom pods, gently crushed
1 small piece fresh gingerroot,
  peeled and minced
1 cup Puy lentils
3 cups vegetable stock
4 firm goat cheeses with rind
  (chèvre), 3½ oz/100 g each
2½ oz/70 g sunblush tomatoes,
  cut into strips
2 tbsp pine nuts, toasted
1 bunch fresh cilantro, leaves only
salt and pepper

# Spiced Lentil Salad with Goat Cheese

You can also serve the lentils cold—just add a little extra olive or walnut oil before serving.

• Heat the oil in a nonstick skillet and cook three-quarters of the onions, the garlic, chili, spices, and ginger, stirring frequently, for 3–5 minutes.

• Add the lentils and stir to coat in the onion mixture, then add the stock and salt and pepper to taste and simmer, stirring occasionally, for 15–20 minutes, or until all the liquid is absorbed and the lentils are tender. Remove the cinnamon stick, star anise, and cardamom pods. Let the lentils cool so that they are warm rather than hot.

• Meanwhile, preheat the broiler to high. Line the broiler pan with foil and brush with a little oil. Place the cheeses in the broiler pan and cook under the broiler until bubbling and brown.

• Divide the lentils between 4 individual plates, then scatter over the remaining onion and top with the tomatoes. Carefully lift the cheeses from the broiler pan and arrange on top of the lentils. Scatter over the pine nuts and the cilantro and serve.

Wherever cheese is produced, it is used in the local cooking, so every country has its traditional recipes that feature its own cheeses. Italy probably uses more cheese in its cooking than any other country, reflecting the importance of agriculture in its history. Its ricotta, Parmesan, and mozzarella cheeses lend themselves very well to a wide variety of dishes, ricotta being particularly versatile since it can be used in both savory and sweet recipes. In addition to the classic cheese and tomato pizza, known as Pizza Margherita, with its traditional mozzarella, we have risotto with creamy bleu Gorgonzola together with the more usual Parmesan, flavored with fresh sage, and homemade ravioli pillows filled with an Italian cheese medley of mozzarella, mascarpone, and Parmesan.

# MAKING A MEAL OF IT

Certain meats seem to have an affinity with a specific cheese, such as Greek halloumi cheese and lamb, as you will discover in the recipe for broiled brochettes, while a bleu cheese sauce really only complements the robust texture and flavor of beef. Bacon and cheese make a sure-fire match, and Tartiflette, a traditional French mountain dish, features lardons or pancetta with mushrooms, potatoes, cream, and Reblochon cheese for a complete meal in itself. There are many classic dishes that pair cheese with shellfish such as crab, lobster, and scallops, as well as with smoked fish, and the soufflé in this chapter combines fresh crabmeat with Gruyère and Parmesan cheese. Nuts and cheese always go well together, and make a great vegetarian team in the Nutty Bleu Cheese Roast.

SERVES 4

2 cups all-purpose flour,
   plus extra for dusting
pinch of salt
2 large eggs
1–2 tbsp olive oil, plus 1 tsp
5½ oz/150 g mozzarella cheese,
   cubed
5½ oz/150 g mascarpone cheese

scant ¾ cup finely grated Parmesan
   cheese, plus extra to serve
1 garlic clove, minced
½ tsp ground nutmeg
scant 4 tbsp butter
½ oz/15 g fresh oregano leaves
⅓ cup pine nuts, toasted
salt and pepper

# Italian Cheese Ravioli with Oregano Butter

This dish has quite a delicate flavor. If you prefer something more robust, replace the mascarpone with a bleu cheese or sharp romano cheese.

• Put the flour and salt in a food processor. Add the eggs and the 1–2 tablespoons of oil and pulse until the mixture just comes together. Turn out onto a lightly floured counter and knead for 2–3 minutes, or until smooth. Wrap the dough in plastic wrap and chill in the refrigerator for 30 minutes.

• Meanwhile, put all the cheeses, garlic, and nutmeg in a large bowl and mash together. Season well with salt and pepper.

• Set a pasta machine to the broadest setting (No 1). Divide the dough into fourths and keep 3 pieces wrapped in plastic wrap while you shape the remaining piece into a rectangle and put through the machine. Fold over, then roll again and continue until you have put the dough through the machine 5 times and the pasta is thin. Cut into thirds and cover with a clean dish towel while you repeat the process with the remaining pasta.

• Cut the pasta into 2¾-inch/7-cm squares. Put a small amount of the cheese filling onto half the squares and moisten the edges of the squares with water. Cover with the remaining pasta squares, expelling all the air, and press the edges firmly together.

• Bring a large pan of water to a boil. Carefully add the ravioli, in batches, then return to a boil and cook for 3 minutes. Meanwhile, melt the butter in a large pan with the remaining oil and the oregano. Remove each batch of ravioli with a slotted spoon when ready, then drain and add to the butter mixture.

• Serve the ravioli scattered with the pine nuts and with extra Parmesan cheese.

SERVES 4

1 cauliflower, about 1 lb 8 oz/675 g
    prepared weight, trimmed and
    cut into florets
1 tbsp olive oil
1 onion, thinly sliced
1 garlic clove, minced
4 oz/115 g lean bacon, cut into
    ½-inch/1-cm strips

3 tbsp butter
3 tbsp all-purpose flour
scant 2 cups milk
4 oz/115 g Cheddar cheese,
    finely grated
a good grating of nutmeg
1 tbsp grated Parmesan cheese
salt and pepper

TO SERVE

tomato or green salad
crusty bread

# Cauliflower and Cheese Casserole

Try using other hard cheeses in this recipe, such as Gruyère or Double Gloucester.

• Preheat the oven to 325°F/160°C. Put an ovenproof serving dish in the oven to warm. Cook the cauliflower in a pan of boiling salted water for 4–5 minutes—it should still be firm. Drain and put in the warmed serving dish, then keep warm in the oven.

• Heat the oil in a skillet and cook the onion, garlic, and bacon, stirring frequently, for 10 minutes, or until the onion is caramelized and golden and the bacon is crisp.

• Melt the butter in a small, heavy-bottom pan and stir in the flour until well combined and smooth. Cook over medium heat, stirring constantly, for 1 minute. Remove from the heat and stir in a little of the milk until well incorporated. Return to the heat and gradually add the remaining milk, stirring constantly, until it has all been incorporated. Cook for an additional 3 minutes, or until the sauce is smooth and thickened. Stir in the Cheddar cheese, nutmeg, and salt and pepper to taste.

• Preheat the broiler to high. Spoon the onion and bacon mixture over the cauliflower and pour over the hot sauce. Sprinkle with the Parmesan cheese and cook under the broiler until browned. Serve immediately with a small tomato or green salad and some crusty bread.

SERVES 4
2½ cups milk
1 onion
8 peppercorns
1 bay leaf
scant 4 tbsp butter
scant ⅓ cup all-purpose flour
½ tsp ground nutmeg
⅓ cup heavy cream

3½ oz/100 g sharp Cheddar cheese,
  grated
3½ oz/100 g Roquefort cheese,
  crumbled
12 oz/350 g dried macaroni
3½ oz/100 g Gruyère or Emmental
  cheese, grated
pepper

# Macaroni Cheese

Many cheeses would work well in this dish—just add your own favorite and perhaps some chopped fresh herbs.

• Put the milk, onion, peppercorns, and bay leaf in a pan and bring to a boil. Remove from the heat and let stand for 15 minutes.
• Melt the butter in a pan and stir in the flour until well combined and smooth. Cook over medium heat, stirring constantly, for 1 minute. Remove from the heat. Strain the milk and stir a little into the butter and flour mixture until well incorporated. Return to the heat and gradually add the remaining milk, stirring constantly, until it has all been incorporated. Cook for an additional 3 minutes, or until the sauce is smooth and thickened, then add the nutmeg, cream, and pepper to taste. Add the Cheddar and Roquefort cheeses and stir until melted.
• Meanwhile, bring a large pan of water to a boil. Add the macaroni, then return to a boil and cook for 8–10 minutes, or until just tender. Drain well and add to the cheese sauce. Stir well together.
• Preheat the broiler to high. Spoon the macaroni cheese into an ovenproof serving dish, then scatter over the Gruyère cheese and cook under the broiler until bubbling and brown.

SERVES 4–6

4 tbsp unsalted butter, plus extra
   for greasing
6 zucchini, sliced
2 tbsp chopped fresh tarragon
   or a mixture of mint, tarragon,
   and flat-leaf parsley

7 oz/200 g Gruyère or Parmesan
   cheese, grated
½ cup milk
½ cup heavy cream
2 eggs
freshly grated nutmeg
salt and pepper

# Zucchini and Cheese Gratin

Gratins are simple vegetable dishes with a bubbling golden topping that are easily adapted to whatever vegetables are available or that you prefer. Although often made with potatoes, this recipe is an example of a lighter custard-based gratin. This dish goes particularly well with roast lamb.

• Preheat the oven to 350°F/180°C. Grease an ovenproof serving dish.

• Melt the butter in a large sauté or skillet and cook the zucchini over medium-high heat, turning occasionally, for 4–6 minutes, or until colored on both sides. Remove from the pan and drain on paper towels, then season to taste with salt and pepper.

• Spread half the zucchini over the bottom of the prepared dish. Sprinkle with half the herbs and 3 oz/85 g of the cheese. Repeat these layers once more.

• Mix the milk, cream, and eggs together in a bowl and add nutmeg and salt and pepper to taste. Pour over the zucchini, then sprinkle with the remaining cheese.

• Bake in the preheated oven for 35–45 minutes, or until set in the center and golden brown on top. Remove from the oven and let stand for 5 minutes before serving straight from the dish.

SERVES 4

12 oz/350 g boneless leg of lamb,
    diced
2 tbsp olive oil
1 tbsp chopped fresh oregano leaves
    or thyme sprigs, plus extra, whole,
    to garnish
finely grated rind of 1 lemon
3 tbsp all-purpose flour

2 eggs, beaten
2 cups fresh white fine bread crumbs
1 large eggplant, sliced into circles
vegetable oil
9 oz/250 g halloumi cheese, cubed
8 bay leaves
1 lemon, cut into fourths
salt and pepper

# Halloumi and Lamb Brochettes with Eggplant Fritters

You can try adding other ingredients to the skewers, such as black olives or cherry tomatoes and squares of red or yellow bell pepper. If you can't find halloumi cheese, use provolone.

• Soak 8 wooden skewers in cold water for 30 minutes. Meanwhile, mix the lamb, olive oil, oregano, and lemon rind together in a bowl. Cover and let chill in the refrigerator for 30 minutes.

• Preheat the oven to 325°F/160°C. Put the flour, eggs, and bread crumbs separately onto 3 plates. Coat each eggplant slice first in the flour, then in the egg, and finally in the bread crumbs.

• Preheat the broiler to high. Heat vegetable oil to a depth of ½ inch/1 cm in a heavy-bottom skillet and cook the eggplant slices, in batches, until crisp on the underside, then turn over and cook on the other side until crisp.

• Remove with a slotted spoon and drain on paper towels. Transfer to a warmed plate and keep warm in the oven while cooking the remaining fritters.

• Pat the lamb dry with paper towels and let return to room temperature. Thread the lamb, cheese, and bay leaves onto the skewers and season to taste with salt and pepper. Cook under the broiler for 4 minutes, then turn the skewers over and cook for an additional 4 minutes, or until the lamb is cooked through and tender.

• Serve 2 skewers for each person with the eggplant fritters and a lemon quarter, garnished with fresh herbs.

SERVES 4
1 lb/450 g loin of pork
2–3 garlic cloves, minced
6 oz/175 g mozzarella di bufala
12 slices prosciutto

12 fresh sage leaves
4 tbsp unsalted butter
salt and pepper
mostarda di Verona, to serve
 (optional)

TO GARNISH
fresh flat-leaf parsley sprigs
lemon slices

# Pan-Fried Pork with Mozzarella

Mostarda di Verona is made with apple purée and is available from some good Italian delicatessens.

• Trim any excess fat from the meat, then slice it crosswise into 12 pieces, each about 1 inch/2.5 cm thick. Stand each piece on end and beat with the flat end of a meat mallet or the side of a rolling pin until thoroughly flattened. Rub each piece all over with the garlic, then transfer to a plate and cover with plastic wrap. Set aside in a cool place for 30 minutes–1 hour.

• Cut the cheese into 12 slices. Season the pork to taste with salt and pepper, then place a slice of cheese on top of each slice of meat. Top with a slice of prosciutto, letting it fall in folds. Place a sage leaf on each portion and secure with a toothpick.

• Melt the butter in a large, heavy-bottom skillet and cook the pork, in batches if necessary, for 2–3 minutes on each side, or until the meat is cooked through and tender and the cheese has melted. Remove with a slotted spoon and keep warm while you cook the remaining pork.

• Remove and discard the toothpicks. Transfer the pork to 4 warmed individual plates, then garnish with the parsley and lemon slices and serve immediately with mostarda di Verona, if you like.

SERVES 4
5 tbsp butter
⅓ cup all-purpose flour
1¼ cups milk
4 eggs, separated
2½ oz/70 g Gruyère cheese, grated

1¾ oz/50 g Parmesan cheese, grated
¼ tsp English mustard powder
7 oz/200 g cooked fresh crabmeat,
    white and brown
salt and pepper

# Crab and Parmesan Soufflé

Fish may be used instead of crab—just make sure it has a strong flavor. Smoked fish works best.

• Preheat the oven to 375°F/190°C. Use 1 tablespoon butter to grease 4 ovenproof, individual serving dishes and chill in the refrigerator.
• Melt the remaining butter in a small, heavy-bottom pan and stir in the flour until well combined and smooth. Cook over medium heat, stirring constantly, for 1 minute. Remove from the heat and stir in a little of the milk until well incorporated. Return to the heat and gradually add the remaining milk, stirring constantly, until it has all been incorporated. Add the egg yolks one at a time and stir well, then add the cheeses and cook for an additional minute, or until the sauce is smooth and thickened.
• Add the mustard, crabmeat, and salt and pepper to taste, then stir well and remove from the heat.
• Whisk the egg whites in a large, grease-free bowl until stiff, then fold in a large spoonful of the crab mixture. Gently fold in the remainder and spoon into the prepared dishes.
• Bake in the preheated oven for 20 minutes, or until puffed up and golden. Serve immediately.

SERVES 6–8

2 tbsp virgin olive oil,
  plus extra for oiling
2 onions
3–5 garlic cloves, crushed
2 celery stalks, finely sliced
6 oz/175 g cooked and peeled
  chestnuts
generous 1 cup mixed chopped nuts

scant 2/3 cup ground almonds
1 cup fresh whole wheat
  bread crumbs
8 oz/225 g bleu cheese, crumbled
1 tbsp chopped fresh basil,
  plus extra sprigs to garnish
1 egg, beaten
1 red bell pepper, peeled, seeded,
  and cut into thin wedges

1 zucchini, about 4 oz/115 g,
  cut into wedges
salt and pepper
cherry tomatoes, to garnish

TO SERVE
tomato sauce
tomato or green salad

# Nutty Bleu Cheese Roast

You can make a quick tomato sauce by cooking a chopped onion and 2 minced garlic cloves in 2 tablespoons olive oil in a pan until soft. Add 14 oz/400 g canned chopped tomatoes and salt and pepper to taste and simmer, covered, for 15 minutes.

• Preheat the oven to 350°F/180°C. Lightly oil a 2-lb/900-g loaf pan.

• Mince one of the onions. Heat half the oil in a skillet and cook the chopped onion, 1–2 of the garlic cloves, and the celery, stirring frequently, for 5 minutes.

• Remove from the pan and drain through a strainer or colander. Transfer to a food processor with the nuts, almonds, bread crumbs, half the cheese, and the basil. Pulse until blended, then pulse again to blend in the egg to form a stiff mixture. Season to taste with salt and pepper.

• Cut the remaining onion into thin wedges. Heat the remaining oil in the skillet and cook the onion wedges, remaining garlic, red bell pepper, and zucchini, stirring frequently, for 5 minutes. Remove from the pan, then drain through a strainer or colander and add salt and pepper to taste.

• Place half the nut mixture in the prepared pan and smooth the surface. Arrange the onion and bell pepper mixture on top and crumble over the remaining cheese. Top with the remaining nut mixture and press down. Cover with foil.

• Bake in the preheated oven for 45 minutes. Remove the foil and bake for an additional 25–35 minutes, or until firm to the touch.

• Let cool for 5 minutes before inverting onto a warmed serving platter. Serve with a little of the tomato sauce (see note) drizzled over the top, garnished with basil sprigs and cherry tomatoes, and accompanied by a salad.

SERVES 4

scant 4 tbsp unsalted butter

6 oz/175 g lardons or pancetta

9 oz/250 g portobello mushrooms, sliced

1 lb 10 oz/750 g waxy potatoes, thinly sliced

9 oz/250 g Reblochon cheese, cubed

2 tbsp fresh tarragon leaves, chopped

1¼ cups heavy cream

salt and pepper

# Tartiflette

This hearty winter dish is traditionally served in France with warm crusty bread and a winter salad. It can also be made in individual pots as a substantial appetizer or lunch.

• Preheat the oven to 325°F/160°C. Use half the butter to grease a 10- x 12-inch/25- x 30-cm baking dish.

• Heat a nonstick skillet and cook the lardons, stirring frequently, over medium-high heat until crisp. Remove with a slotted spoon and drain on paper towels.

• Add the mushrooms to the skillet and cook, stirring frequently, for 5 minutes. Remove with a slotted spoon and drain on paper towels.

• Season the potato slices to taste with salt and pepper and arrange half in the prepared baking dish. Top with the lardons and mushrooms, half the cheese, and the tarragon. Top with the remaining potatoes, then pour over the cream and dot with the remaining butter.

• Bake in the preheated oven for 1¼ hours. Scatter over the remaining cheese and bake for an additional 15 minutes, or until the cheese is bubbling and brown. Remove from the oven, cover lightly with foil, and let rest for 10 minutes before serving.

SERVES 2

DOUGH

1½ cups all-purpose flour,
  plus extra for dusting

1 tsp salt

1 tsp active dry yeast

1 tbsp olive oil, plus extra for oiling

6 tbsp lukewarm water

TOPPING

6 tomatoes, thinly sliced

6 oz/175 g mozzarella cheese,
  thinly sliced

2 tbsp shredded fresh basil leaves

2 tbsp olive oil

salt and pepper

# Cheese and Tomato Pizza

To make a Pizza Napoletana, first spread each pizza base with 4½ teaspoons tomato paste, then top with the tomato and cheese slices. Arrange drained and halved canned anchovy fillets in a pattern on top and season to taste with pepper, then drizzle with olive oil and bake the pizza as in the main recipe.

• To make the dough, sift the flour and salt into a bowl and stir in the yeast. Make a well in the center. Add the oil and water to the well. Using a wooden spoon or floured hands, gradually incorporate the dry ingredients into the liquid to form a dough.
• Turn the dough out onto a lightly floured counter and knead well for 5 minutes, or until smooth and elastic. Return the dough to the cleaned bowl, then cover with lightly oiled plastic wrap and let stand in a warm place to rise for 1 hour, or until doubled in size.
• Preheat the oven to 450°F/230°C. Lightly oil a cookie sheet. Turn the dough out onto the lightly floured counter and knock back. Knead briefly, then cut in half and roll out each piece into a circle about ¼ inch/5 mm thick. Transfer to the prepared cookie sheet and push up the edges with your fingers to form a small rim.
• To make the topping, arrange the tomato and mozzarella slices alternately over the dough circles. Season to taste with salt and pepper, sprinkle with the basil, and drizzle with the oil.
• Bake the pizza in the preheated oven for 15–20 minutes, or until the crust is crisp and the cheese has melted. Serve immediately.

SERVES 4

scant 4 tbsp unsalted butter
5½ oz/150 g pancetta, cubed
1 small onion, chopped
2 garlic cloves, crushed
scant 1½ cups risotto rice
½ cup white wine or vermouth

4 cups hot chicken or vegetable stock
7 oz/200 g Gorgonzola cheese,
   crumbled
2 tbsp minced fresh sage, plus extra,
   whole, to garnish
2 tbsp finely grated Parmesan cheese
salt and pepper

# Sage and Gorgonzola Risotto

To make risotto cakes, simply let the risotto cool completely, then add 2 tablespoons all-purpose flour and 1 small egg yolk, mix well, and form into flat cakes. Cook in hot oil until golden and serve with asparagus spears and fresh Parmesan cheese shavings.

• Heat half the butter in a large pan or skillet and cook the pancetta over medium-high heat, stirring frequently, until the fat melts and the pancetta is beginning to brown. Add the onion and garlic and cook, stirring frequently, for 5 minutes, or until the onion is soft.

• Add the rice and stir to coat in the pancetta mixture. Pour in the wine and cook, stirring constantly, until almost all the liquid has been absorbed. Start to add the hot stock, a ladleful at a time, stirring constantly and letting each addition be absorbed before adding the next. Continue adding the stock until it is all absorbed and the rice is creamy but still firm to the bite.

• Remove from the heat, then add the Gorgonzola cheese and sage and stir until the cheese has melted. Season to taste with salt and pepper and add the remaining butter and the Parmesan cheese. Serve immediately garnished with sage.

Cheese is a wonderful addition in baking, including bread and biscuits. Many traditional loaves work well with the addition of cubed or grated cheese, and melting cheeses such as Taleggio and fontina are delicious half kneaded into and half scattered over foccacia—the recipe here also includes olives and fresh rosemary for extra flavor. Spices such as paprika, celery salt, and mustard powder will also enhance the flavor of cheese in baking.

Cheesecake is probably the first dessert that springs to mind when it comes to cheese in sweet dishes, but there are many others using cheese. Mascarpone, curd, cream, and ricotta cheese—the latter used in the cheesecake recipe here—are employed most often because they have a creamy consistency and a mild flavor that doesn't overpower the other ingredients. Ricotta also

# TREAT YOURSELF

features in this chapter as a sumptuous filling for a Genoa sponge cake, mixed with chocolate, cream, and candied peel, and sweetened and combined with dried fruit, orange rind, and cinnamon to make delicious individual desserts. With the addition of some sugar and vanilla, and perhaps a little liqueur, mascarpone can be used instead of cream in trifles and as a topping for tarts, pies, or desserts. It also makes wonderful ice cream. Here it stars in the mousselike Mascarpone Creams, together with crushed amaretti cookies soaked in amaretto for a hint of almond, and the Italian answer to trifle—a luxurious tiramisù with an extra hazelnut dimension.

SERVES 4

1 tsp butter

2/3 cup all-purpose flour

1 tbsp baking powder

pinch of salt

3½ oz/100 g polenta/ground maize

1 cup grated sharp Cheddar cheese

2 eggs, beaten

1¼ cups whole milk

scant 4 tbsp butter, melted

# Cheddar Corn Bread

To use as a topping for chili con carne, crumble the corn bread into rough crumbs, add a handful of grated cheese and brown under the broiler.

• Preheat the oven to 400°F/200°C. Use the butter to grease a 4-cup loaf pan and line the base with waxed paper.

• Mix the flour, baking powder, salt, and polenta together in a large bowl. Stir in the cheese. Make a well in the center. Add the eggs, milk, and butter to the well. Using a wooden spoon, gradually incorporate the dry ingredients into the liquid until smooth.

• Pour the mixture into the prepared pan and bake in the preheated oven for 40–45 minutes, or until risen, golden, and firm to the touch.

• Let cool in the pan for 10 minutes before turning out onto a cooling rack to cool completely.

• Cut into thick slices to serve warm or cold.

SERVES 4

1 lb 2 oz/500 g white bread flour,
    plus extra for dusting
1 envelope active dry yeast
1 tsp superfine sugar
1¼ cups warm water

5 tbsp olive oil, plus extra for oiling
12 green olives, pitted
7 oz/200 g fontina cheese, cubed
2 fresh rosemary sprigs, leaves only
salt

# Foccacia with Fontina Cheese and Green Olives

Black olives and sun-dried tomatoes also work well in this bread, or add a scattering of sautéed red onion slices.

• Sift the flour into a large bowl and stir in 1 teaspoon salt and the yeast. Make a well in the center. Mix the sugar and water together in a pitcher, stirring until the sugar has dissolved. Add to the well with 1 tablespoon of the oil. Using a wooden spoon or floured hands, gradually incorporate the dry ingredients into the liquid to form a dough.
• Turn the dough out onto a lightly floured counter and knead for 5 minutes, or until smooth and elastic. Transfer the dough to a lightly oiled bowl. Cover with plastic wrap and let stand in a warm place to rise for 2 hours.
• Meanwhile, heat 1 tablespoon of the remaining oil in a pan and cook the olives over low heat, stirring, for 2–3 minutes. Let cool.
• Lightly oil a cookie sheet. Turn out the dough onto the counter and knead in the olives and half the cheese. Pull the dough gently into a shape measuring about 14-inch/35-cm square and place on the prepared cookie sheet. Cover with a clean dish towel and let stand in a warm place for 1 hour.
• Meanwhile, preheat the oven to 400°F/200°C. Sprinkle the dough with the remaining oil and scatter over the rosemary. Bake in the preheated oven for 15 minutes. Press the remaining cheese into the loaf and scatter over salt to taste. Reduce the oven temperature to 375°F/190°C and bake for an additional 15 minutes.
• Let cool on a cooling rack and serve warm or cold.

MAKES 8

3 tbsp butter, diced and chilled, plus extra for greasing

generous ¾ cup white self-rising flour, plus extra for dusting

generous ¾ cup whole wheat self-rising flour

1 tsp baking powder

pinch of salt

generous ¾ cup finely grated Cheddar cheese

2 tbsp snipped fresh chives, plus extra to garnish

3 tbsp milk

# Cheese and Chive Biscuits

Choose a sharp, well-flavored Cheddar cheese for these biscuits, to give them a strong, well-rounded taste.

• Preheat the oven to 425°F/220°C. Grease a cookie sheet.

• Sift the flours, baking powder, and salt into a bowl. Add the butter and rub in with your fingertips until the mixture resembles fine bread crumbs. Stir in ¹/₂ cup of the cheese and the chives. Add up to 1 tablespoon of the milk and mix to form a fairly soft, light dough.

• Turn the dough out onto a lightly floured counter and roll out to ³/₄ inch/2 cm thick. Using a 2¹/₂-inch/6-cm plain cookie cutter, stamp out circles and place on the prepared cookie sheet. Reroll the trimmings and stamp out more circles until the dough is used up. Brush the tops with the remaining milk and sprinkle with the remaining cheese.

• Bake the biscuits in the preheated oven for 10 minutes, or until well risen and golden. Let cool on a cooling rack. Garnish with chives and serve warm or cold.

SERVES 4

2 large eggs, beaten,
    plus 1 medium egg

2/3 cup milk

4 tbsp water

pinch of salt

6 tbsp all-purpose flour

7/8 stick butter, melted,
    plus extra for greasing

1 1/8 cups curd cheese

scant 1/2 cup ricotta cheese

scant 1 cup cream cheese

1/4 cup superfine sugar

1 vanilla bean, split and
    seeds removed

1/2 tsp orange flower water

1 cup fresh blackberries

1 tbsp crème de cassis

1 tbsp confectioners' sugar

1/2 tsp ground cinnamon

1 cup sour cream

# Cheese Blintzes

This is a rich dessert and the blackberries make a good contrast to the richness of the cheese crêpes, but you could use other fruits such as cranberries or black currants.

• Whisk the 2 large eggs with the milk and water in a large bowl and add the salt. Add the flour a spoonful at a time, beating after each addition, until you have a batter.

• Pour the batter through a strainer into a pitcher and let stand for 20 minutes.

• Preheat the oven to 375°F/190°C. Heat a little of the butter in an 8-inch/20-cm nonstick skillet and add just enough batter to cover the bottom of the skillet. Cook until the underside is golden brown and the crêpe is beginning to color at the edge. Slide the crêpe onto a piece of waxed paper. Repeat with the remaining batter, adding a little more of the remaining butter as necessary.

• Beat the cheeses, remaining egg, sugar, seeds from the vanilla bean, and the flower water together in a large bowl until well combined.

• Grease a ceramic baking dish. Take each crêpe and spoon some filling into the center. Fold the crêpe over and then over again to form a triangle.

• Arrange the blintzes, overlapping, in the prepared dish. Brush over the remaining butter and bake in the preheated oven for 15–20 minutes.

• Meanwhile, put the blackberries and crème de cassis in a pan and heat until the fruits are well covered and sticky. Set aside.

• To serve, sift the confectioners' sugar and cinnamon over the blintzes and serve with the sour cream and a spoonful of the blackberries.

SERVES 4

4 oz/115 g amaretti cookies, crushed

4 tbsp amaretto or maraschino

4 eggs, separated

¼ cup superfine sugar

1 cup mascarpone cheese

toasted slivered almonds, to decorate

## Mascarpone Creams

The easiest way to make biscuit crumbs is to put the cookies in a plastic bag and crush with a rolling pin.

• Put the amaretti crumbs in a bowl, then add the amaretto and set aside to soak.

• Meanwhile, beat the egg yolks with the sugar in a separate bowl until pale and thick. Fold in the mascarpone and soaked amaretti crumbs.

• Whisk the egg whites in a separate, grease-free bowl until stiff peaks form, then gently fold into the cheese mixture. Divide the mixture between 4 serving dishes and chill in the refrigerator for 1–2 hours. Sprinkle with slivered almonds just before serving.

SERVES 4–6

¾ cup cold espresso or
   strong black coffee
⅓ cup Kahlúa
scant ¼ cup superfine sugar
3 eggs, separated
1 lb 2 oz/500 g mascarpone cheese

½ tsp vanilla extract
7 oz/200 g ladyfingers
1¾ oz/50 g amaretti cookies, crushed
⅔ cup hazelnuts, toasted
   and chopped
1 oz/25 g unsweetened cocoa

# Hazelnut Tiramisù

Instead of unsweetened cocoa, you can scatter crushed hazelnut praline or honeycomb on top of the tiramisù.

• Mix the coffee and Kahlúa together in a shallow dish.
• Whisk the sugar and egg yolks together in a large bowl until pale and mousselike, then beat in the cheese and vanilla extract.
• Whisk the egg whites in a separate large, grease-free bowl until stiff peaks form, then fold these into the cheese mixture.
• Smear 1–2 spoonfuls of the mousse over the bottom of 4–6 individual serving dishes and then begin to dip the ladyfingers into the coffee mixture. Don't leave in the liquid or they will disintegrate—dip them just long enough until the sponge begins to soften between your fingers. Make a layer of the dipped ladyfingers on top of the mousse and scatter over some of the amaretti crumbs and the hazelnuts.
• Keep layering the mousse with the sponge fingers, amaretti crumbs, and nuts, finishing with a layer of mousse. Cover with plastic wrap and chill in the refrigerator overnight.
• Just before serving, sift over unsweetened cocoa to cover the top.

SERVES 4
1 tbsp butter
2¾ oz/75 g mixed dried fruit
1⅛ cups ricotta cheese
3 egg yolks

¼ cup superfine sugar
1 tsp ground cinnamon
finely grated rind of 1 orange,
    plus extra to decorate
crème fraîche or sour cream, to serve

# Tuscan Desserts

Crème fraîche is suitable for cooking as it has the same fat content as heavy cream. It can be made by stirring cultured buttermilk into heavy cream and chilling overnight.

• Preheat the oven to 350°F/180°C. Lightly grease 4 mini ovenproof bowls or ramekins with the butter.
• Put the dried fruit in a bowl and cover with warm water. Let soak for 10 minutes.
• Beat the cheese with the egg yolks in a separate bowl. Stir in the sugar, cinnamon, and orange rind and mix well. Drain the dried fruit in a strainer set over a bowl. Mix the drained fruit with the ricotta cheese mixture. Spoon the mixture into the prepared basins or ramekins.
• Bake the desserts in the preheated oven for 15 minutes. The tops should be firm to the touch but not browned.
• Turn the desserts out onto individual serving plates and decorate with orange rind. Serve warm or chilled with a spoonful of crème fraîche or sour cream.

SERVES 6–8

PIE DOUGH

scant 1¼ cups all-purpose flour,
  plus extra for dusting

3 tbsp superfine sugar

pinch of salt

1 stick unsalted butter,
  diced and chilled

1 egg yolk

FILLING

1 lb/450 g ricotta cheese

½ cup heavy cream

2 eggs, plus 1 egg yolk

scant ½ cup superfine sugar

finely grated rind of 1 lemon

finely grated rind of 1 orange

# Ricotta Cheesecake

You can decorate the top of the cheesecake before serving with finely pared strips of lemon and orange rind.

• To make the pie dough, sift the flour, sugar, and salt onto a counter and make a well in the center. Add the butter and egg yolk to the well. Using your fingertips, gradually work in the flour mixture until fully incorporated.

• Gather up the dough and knead very lightly. Cut off about one-quarter, then wrap in plastic wrap and chill in the refrigerator. Press the remaining dough into the bottom of a 9-inch/23-cm, loose-bottom tart pan. Chill in the refrigerator for 30 minutes.

• To make the filling, beat all the ingredients together in a bowl. Cover with plastic wrap and chill in the refrigerator until required.

• Preheat the oven to 375°F/190°C. Prick the base of the pastry shell all over with a fork. Line with foil, then fill with dried beans and bake blind in the preheated oven for 15 minutes.

• Remove the foil and beans and let the pan cool on a cooling rack.

• Spoon the ricotta mixture into the pastry shell and smooth the surface. Roll out the reserved pastry on a lightly floured counter and cut into strips. Arrange the strips over the filling in a lattice pattern, brushing the overlapping ends with water so that they stick.

• Bake in the oven for 30–35 minutes, or until the top of the cheesecake is golden and the filling has set. Let cool on a cooling rack before lifting off the side of the pan. Cut into wedges to serve.

SERVES 4

Genoa sponge cake

6 eggs, separated

generous ½ cup superfine sugar

generous ½ cup self-rising flour

⅔ cup cornstarch

FILLING

1 lb 2 oz/500 g ricotta cheese

1 cup superfine sugar

2½ cups maraschino

3 squares bittersweet chocolate

7 oz/200 g mixed candied peel, diced

1¼ cups heavy cream

TO DECORATE

candied cherries

angelica

candied fruit

slivered almonds

# Sicilian Ice Cream Cake

Maraschino is a sweet, colorless liqueur made from fermented bitter maraschino cherries. If you prefer, you can use orange-flavored Cointreau.

• Preheat the oven to 350°F/180°C. Line a 10-inch/25-cm springform cake pan with parchment paper.

• To make the sponge cake, beat the egg yolks with the sugar in a large bowl until pale and frothy. Whisk the egg whites in a separate, large grease-free bowl until stiff peaks form. Gently fold the egg whites into the egg yolk mixture with a figure-eight action.

• Sift the flour and cornstarch together into another bowl, then sift into the egg mixture and gently fold in. Pour the batter into the prepared cake pan and smooth the surface. Bake in the preheated oven for 30 minutes, or until springy to the touch. Turn out onto a cooling rack, then remove the lining paper and let cool completely.

• To make the filling, put the cheese, sugar, and 1¾ cups of the maraschino in a bowl and beat together well. Chop the chocolate with a knife and stir into the mixture with the candied peel.

• Cut the sponge cake into strips about ½ inch/1 cm wide and use to line the bottom and sides of a 2-lb/900-g loaf pan. Set aside the remaining slices.

• Spoon the ricotta cheese mixture into the pan and smooth the surface. Cover with the reserved strips of sponge cake. Drizzle the remaining maraschino over the top, then cover and chill in the refrigerator overnight.

• Run a round-bladed knife around the sides of the pan and turn out onto a serving plate. Whip the cream in a bowl until stiff peaks form. Coat the top and sides of the cake with the cream and decorate with the cherries, angelica, candied fruit, and almonds.

Although there is a bewilderingly wide range of cheeses on offer, they do actually fall broadly into five groups:

**Soft-Paste:** These soft, pliable cheeses have unwashed rinds and include Camembert, Brie, and Reblochon.

**Medium-Soft:** Slightly firmer than the previous group with a moist rind, such as Pont l'Evêque and Taleggio.

**Hard Cheese:** These range from the hardest, crumbly cheese, such as Parmesan and romano, to slightly more pliable but still firm cheeses, such as many English cheeses, including Cheddar, Leicester, and Double Gloucester.

**Bleu Cheese:** These can be soft and creamy like Gorgonzola or firm and crumbly like Stilton—it's the distinctive flavor that counts.

**Soft Cheeses:** These are often made from goat milk and can be medium-soft with a soft rind, such as French chèvre, right through to the freshest soft curd cheeses with a milky, mild taste.

# Cheeseboard

A good cheeseboard offers a selection of cheeses with good contrasts of flavor and texture. A choice of between five or six cheeses should provide something for everyone, from a strongly flavored hard cheese to a mild, milky soft cheese.

• Make your cheeseboard inviting by buying a good variety of cheeses of different shapes, sizes, textures, and colors, and try to include one cheese from each of the above groups. Always have decent-size pieces of cheese rather than lots of small pieces—it is better to have two or three substantial wedges than ten small bits, or, at Christmas, just have a whole Stilton. A couple of ash-mold whole goat cheeses will contrast nicely with some wedges of hard cheese and a good slice of something soft and squidgy. Some farmhouse and artisan cheeses are season specific, so do look out for these when available and make the most of any local producers.

• Make sure you take your cheese out of the refrigerator well ahead of when you plan to serve it, in order to take off the chill and enable the cheese to come up to room temperature to make the best of its taste, smell, and texture.

• Be creative about what you offer alongside the cheeseboard. Apart from the obvious water biscuits and oatcakes, have fresh, crusty bread or walnut bread and perhaps Italian flatbreads. Fruit goes very well with cheese, as do nuts, so offer something unusual such as Medjhool dates and walnuts or membrillo (quince paste) and almonds. Figs and Cape gooseberries as well as perfectly ripe pears and crunchy apples are wonderful with cheese, not forgetting grapes and celery, the traditional accompaniments for cheese, ever popular because they do complement it so well. Fruitcake, dried vine fruits, and sweetened chestnuts are delicious with well-flavored hard cheeses, and a little honey drizzled over mild, fresh goat cheese is very good. You can also roll bite-size balls of goat cheese in chopped nuts or chopped fresh herbs or ground spices.